*"There has never been a more urgent need to revive damaged ecosystems than now"*

*– UN Decade on Ecosystem Restoration (2021-30)*

INDIA • SINGAPORE • MALAYSIA

http://www.junglescapes.org

# REVIVING WILDLIFE HABITATS

## A FIELD MANUAL FOR ECOLOGICAL RESTORATION OF FORESTS INVADED BY *LANTANA CAMARA*

# CONTENTS

*"Alien invasive species may be as damaging to native species and ecosystems on a global scale as the loss and degradation of habitats"*

*- International Union for Conservation of Nature*

# FOREWORD

We are endowed with great wildlife and large tracts of forest. Despite huge anthropogenic pressure on our natural ecosystems, we have successfully protected and conserved our forests and wildlife and in some cases revived some of our threatened key species. India has some of the greatest conservation stories in the world and yet everything is not alright deep within the forests.

The menace of invasive weeds is threatening to destroy the forests like never before. The quality of ground and middle-story vegetation in our sanctuaries and parks is seriously getting affected by weeds like *Lantana camara*. This has limited the availability of palatable grasses and herbs and downgraded the habitat for various animals; depriving the herbivores of quality forage. There is an urgent need to tackle this problem before it assumes monstrous proportions. The less availability of grasses and bamboo (in Karnataka in particular because of bamboo flowering) could lead to animals straying out in search of food resulting in increased incidents of human-animal conflict. Eventually, it could reduce the density of herbivores in our sanctuaries with negative consequences on the carnivore population.

Junglescapes has taken up this challenging task of Lantana removal and post-removal ecological restoration on established scientific methods under an MOU with the Karnataka Forest Department. The cut-rootstock method of removal followed by restoration and maintenance appears to be a very effective way for Lantana eradication. This field manual is the result of their work in Bandipur National Park in the last decade over an area of over 600 hectares and holds great promise in our fight against Lantana and other weeds. Lantana removal cannot be a one-time effort. It has to be a sustained effort over an area to make sure that the Lantana and other secondary weeds do not come back easily. This has been brought out clearly in the manual.

The Karnataka Forest Department has also started taking up the removal of Lantana over large tracts of protected areas using NREGA funds. The valuable suggestions from this field manual should be incorporated in the action plan of the department for better results.

To conclude, this is a huge challenge as Lantana and a few other weeds have occupied and encroached on large chunks of forest land threatening their quality, productivity and biodiversity. More and more efforts are needed to develop best practice methods for weed eradication and I wish more areas could be taken by Junglescapes in different forest types where Lantana is prevalent. Our forests have to be made Lantana-free at any cost.

13th December 2023

Sanjai Mohan IFS
PCCF & Hoff (retd.)
Karnataka Forest Department

# PREFACE

Degradation of forest ecosystems has emerged as a major concern in India and around the world. The rapid spread of invasive alien plant species has been identified as one of the major factors leading to the degradation of forest habitats. As a result, while overall forest cover has been seen to be improving in India, the health of the forests is a cause for concern. Many Protected Areas remain legally protected but ecologically threatened. While one sees significant efforts towards the conservation of endangered faunal species, these cannot succeed unless the habitats of these species are healthy. Conservation and ecological restoration are, therefore, two sides of the same coin and have to be addressed simultaneously.

Junglescapes is one of the pioneers in South India in the field of ecological restoration of forest areas impacted by invasive alien species like *Lantana camara*. Our efforts since 2014, in collaboration with the Karnataka Forest Department, have resulted in the revival of native biodiversity in over 600 hectares of forests that were occupied by *Lantana camara* and other associated invasive alien plant species. These wildlife habitats have witnessed good rewilding by almost all taxa of representative fauna.

This field manual is based on our experience gained over the last 10 years in the restoration of *Lantana camara*-invaded landscapes. This manual aims to share our learnings with a wider audience in India and abroad who may wish to use them in their restoration efforts, with or without contextual modifications.

Our managing trustee, Mr Ramesh Venkataraman, is a member of the Expert Committee on Invasive Species appointed by the Hon'ble High Court of Madras in 2019. Some of the material featured in this manual has also been contributed by him to the expert committee's report.

The primary role in managing *Lantana camara* in protected forests of India is with the forest departments of the respective States. We sincerely hope this field manual will be of use to the different forest departments in India.

There is a widespread view that managing *Lantana camara* is not feasible in India as it has spread over vast tracts of our forests. Our experience indicates that with a strategic long-term approach, we can retrieve much of our native biodiversity over the next two decades. This field manual is our contribution towards this ambitious goal.

Junglescapes Charitable Trust<br>
Bangalore<br>
July 2024

# ACKNOWLEDGEMENTS

We would like to express our sincere gratitude to the Karnataka Forest Department for their continuous support of our efforts.

Our sincere thanks to Sri Sanjai Mohan IFS, Principal Chief Conservator of Forests and Hoff (Retd.), Karnataka Forest Department, for writing a foreword to this manual. His encouragement and guidance were instrumental in our restoration efforts in Bandipur Tiger Reserve in Karnataka.

We are grateful to Prof Dr C.R. Babu and Dr Rakesh Dahiya of CEMDE, New Delhi for their valuable guidance and inputs to our Lantana management programme.

We would like to thank the CEPF-ATREE Western Ghats program which helped us embark on our efforts on Lantana management. A special word of thanks is due to Dr Siddappa Setty of ATREE for the mentorship he provided us during our formative years.

Our active involvement with the Society for Ecological Restoration has helped us adopt sound restoration principles and methodologies, as well as global best practices.

Ecological restoration is a long-term exercise. The sustained support of our institutional sponsors and individual donors has been vital and we are very grateful to all of them. The continued funding and employee volunteering support from GE India since the commencement of our restoration activities in 2009 has been pivotal in helping us gradually scale up our efforts.

We thank our trustees, Project Governance Committee members and volunteers who, over the years, have contributed their time and expertise towards our projects. We would also like to thank all our staff members who have travelled the unchartered road of ecological restoration with a high level of commitment and perseverance.

We thank institutions such as AERF, FRLHT, French Institute of Pondicherry, KFRI and Arulagam that have readily shared their knowledge with us from time to time. We also thank Mr R Sundararaju IFS, PCCF (Retd.) of the Tamil Nadu Forest Department, for sharing insights from his long experience in dealing with invasive species.

This manual has been prepared by Mr Ramesh Venkataraman, our Managing Trustee. He is a member of the UN-FAO Task Force on Best Practices for the UN Decade on Ecosystem Restoration. He is also a member of the Expert Committee on Invasive Species appointed by the Hon'ble High Court of Madras. Inputs to this manual have been provided by Dr DL Shrisha, Dr K Anand, Mr CR Hanumanth, Mr CH Sathisha and Mr Kaustubh Moghe. Mr KN Mahesha provided many of the photographs. We thankfully acknowledge their efforts.

Junglescapes follows a model of restoration that encourages communities living adjacent to forests to participate actively in the restoration initiatives. Hence, last but not least, we would like to thank the community members that we partner with, mostly indigenous, living at the periphery of Bandipur National Park. The restoration efforts and outcomes would have been impossible without their involvement and the traditional ecological knowledge contributed by them. They are the true heroes of the efforts of a decade and a half to restore biodiversity to these crucial wildlife habitats.

Junglescapes Charitable Trust
Bangalore
July 2024

## WE THANK OUR INSTITUTIONAL SPONSORS

**... AND MANY INDIVIDUAL DONORS ...**

***whose support over the years has made the restoration of Lantana-invaded wildlife habitats possible***

CHAPTER 1

# BACKGROUND

## 1.1 INTRODUCTION

*Lantana camara* is considered to be one of the top 10 invasive plant species in the world. Native to South America, it has now spread to many continents, including Asia, Australia and Africa, where it is considered an invasive alien species (IAS). In India, it is believed to have been introduced as an ornamental plant by the British around 1805 in Kolkatta. Since then it has spread across India and adapted to multiple geographic and climatic zones. As a result, many of the natural ecosystems across the country have been severely impacted by the spread of *Lantana camara*, and it has become a major threat to biodiversity and the provision of ecosystem services. Importantly, the weed has led to high degradation of wildlife habitats, posing a threat to the conservation of many important plant and animal species.

## 1.2 DESCRIPTION

*Lantana camara* is a medium-sized perennial, aromatic shrub, 2-5m tall, with quadrangular stems, sometimes having prickles. The posture may be sub-erect, scrambling, or occasionally as climbers. Frequently, multiple stems arise from ground level. The leaves are generally oval or broadly lance-shaped, 2-12cm in length, and 2-6 cm broad, having a rough surface and a yellow-green to green colour. The inflorescence may be yellow, orange, white, pale violet, pink or red (refer to Figure 1). Flowers are small, multi-coloured, in stalked, flat-topped clusters up to 4 cm across. Fruits are round and fleshy and about 5 mm wide, green turning purple then blue-black (refer to Figure 2)

Figure 1: *Lantana camara* inflorescence and leaf pattern

Figure 2: *Lantana camara* fruits in the process of ripening (Shutterstock image)

The taxonomic classification of *L. camara* is as below:

| | | |
|---|---|---|
| Class | : | Dicotyledonae |
| Order | : | Lamiales |
| Family | : | Verbenaceae |
| Genus | : | *Lantana* |
| Species | : | *Lantana camara* L. |
| Common name | : | Common Lantana, Wild sage |

Note:

The species is referred to as *Lantana camara* or by its common name 'Lantana' in this field manual. However, there is a species of the Lantana genus native to India, namely *Lantana indica* (Refer to Figure 3) , which is not considered an invasive species in India.

Figure 3: *Lantana indica* inflorescence

## 1.3 DISTRIBUTION

The diverse and broad geographic distribution of Lantana camara is a reflection of its wide ecological tolerance[1]. It occurs in a variety of forest types ranging from moist deciduous forests (e.g. parts of Nagarhole and Corbett Tiger Reserves), semi-arid forests (e.g. Sasan Gir National Park), dry deciduous forests (e.g. parts of Bandipur and Mudumalai Tiger Reserves) and many tropical thorn scrub jungles of peninsular India.

It can grow in a variety of soil types, elevations and rainfall conditions but functions best in open areas with more sunlight. It does not tolerate saline or dry soils, water logging or low temperatures (<5 degrees C)[2]. Earlier seen only at lower altitudes, the species can now be observed at higher altitudes of up to 2,000 m. It now grows around towns like Coonoor (1,650 m) and Kothagiri (1,950 m) in the Nilgiris.

Importantly, the species is found to be growing profusely in non-forest areas e.g. fallow agricultural lands, alongside highways and railway tracks, fringe areas of cities and towns, etc.

## 1.4 INVASIVE CHARACTERISTICS

*Lantana camara* has multiple invasive characteristics that make it an aggressive coloniser. These are described below:

a. The plant flowers throughout the year with a peak during the first two months of the rainy season.
b. Lantana produces a huge number of seeds each year. Plants reach maturity in a short period and each mature plant can produce over 12,000 seeds a year[3]. Long seed viability estimated at over 10 years results in the build-up of large sub-soil seed banks which become active with any soil disturbance.

---

1 Refer Annexure 5 for citation details
2 Refer Annexure 5 for citation details
3 Refer Annexure 5 for citation details

c. The plant deploys multiple barrier mechanisms that inhibit the establishment of other competing flora (refer to Figure 4)

- Being an allelopathic plant, Lantana releases chemical compounds into the surrounding soil. This prevents the establishment of native plant species, thereby eliminating competition for resources (chemical barrier).
- The large umbrella-like crown creates a closed canopy. This prevents seeds of taller plant species from falling to the ground resulting in low recruitment. For example, areas with high Lantana invasions have witnessed low regeneration of tall keystone species like *Bambusa bambos*. The umbrella-like canopy also deprives seeds and seedlings of native plants of sunlight essential for their establishment (seed and light barriers).
- Shallow and well-spread lateral roots close to the soil surface help Lantana scavenge and monopolise nutrients over a large area and reduce nutrient availability for native plant species (nutrient barrier).

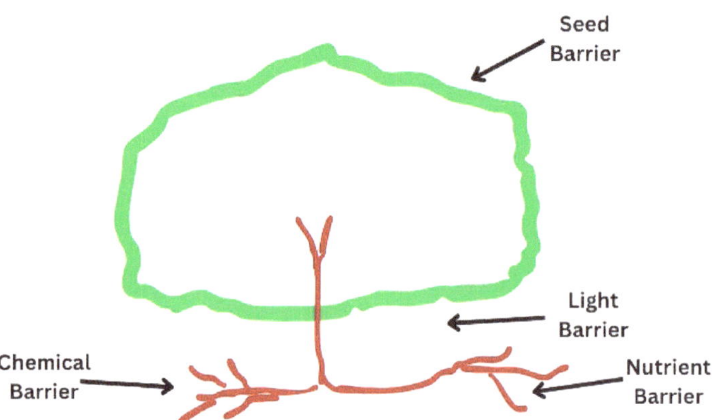


Figure 4: Multiple barriers to native vegetation deployed by *Lantana camara*

d. The plant has multiple seed dispersal mechanisms. Birds like Bulbuls are the main dispersal agents. Water is another important dispersal route, indicated by higher levels of invasion at foothills and stream banks.

e. The plant can also take root from stem cuttings, a reproductive mechanism called layering. Layering is a form of vegetative propagation where stems send roots into the soil, allowing them to quickly form very dense stands and spread short distances[4]. However, Lantana does not regenerate from root fragments ("suckering").
f. Lantana is considered a fire-loving species since fire breaks the dormancy of sub-soil seeds leading to intense re-invasion through fresh recruitment.
g. The weed is well adapted to fires. After the forest fires in Bandipur National Park in 2019, it was observed that almost 90% of the Lantana shrubs in fire-affected areas were re-coppicing aggressively from the base (basal coppicing), although the above-ground portions were fully burnt (refer to Figure 16 on page 42).
h. The species quickly invades areas with anthropogenic disturbance e.g. fires, use of earth-moving equipment to clear forest patches, infrastructural activities like road-making, etc.
i. Lantana is very long-lived under favourable conditions. Constantly renewed growth at the base of the stems ensures its persistence. Plants tend to die only under extremely stressful conditions, such as extended drought or complete shading through canopy closure[5].

## 1.5 ECOSYSTEM IMPACTS

*Lantana camara* has numerous and far-reaching adverse consequences to ecosystem functioning, diversity and succession.

a. The invasive characteristics of the plant enable it to spread rapidly and occupy large forest areas in a short period of time.

---

4 Refer Annexure 5 for citation details
5 Refer Annexure 5 for citation details

Native plant species, particularly those forming the under-storey vegetation, are therefore pushed out due to the lack of space and nutrition needed for regeneration.

b. As discussed in Para 1.4, Lantana uses multiple 'barriers' to severely impair the recruitment and establishment of other plant species. As a result, invaded areas present a picture of an ageing forest with Lantana and surviving adult native trees, with no succession (refer to Figure 5). There is near-total elimination of under-storey plant habits like grasses, shrubs and herbs. Species richness and abundance, and plant community compositions, are severely impacted.

Figure 5: Typical Lantana invaded area with a few adult trees and no succession

c. By completely occupying the bottom and middle storeys of the forest, Lantana leads to significant impairment of structural diversity of vegetation as well as the disappearance of ecological niches. This has far-reaching impacts on a wide diversity of fauna that occupy different structural zones and niches in a forest.

d. Lantana-occupied forests see a gradual decline in the abundance of browsing/palatable plant species due to their over-exploitation by herbivores in the absence of adequate fodder. This often leads to a highly imbalanced plant community composition, dominated by Lantana and non-browsable native plant species.
e. The plant leads to a significant decline in diversity and abundance of insect species, which form the foundation of the ecosystem. This combined with a reduction in grass and shrub abundance leads to soil degradation and impairment of hydrological cycles.
f. The leaves and seeds of the plant have been observed to harbour toxic compounds. The plant is thus not palatable for herbivores. Experiments in Australia with kangaroos have shown severe damage to internal organs when fed with Lantana leaves[6]. Lantana poisoning also takes a heavy toll on livestock[7]. Although grazing animals primarily do not consume this plant, scarcity of pasture lands causes the animals to eat this plant. Consumption of this plant causes hepatotoxicity and secondary photosensitisation in animals[8].
g. Contiguous thickets of Lantana that become dry in summer significantly increase the risk of fast-moving forest fires thanks to its high calorific value. Compared to fires in grasslands which generally are low-height fires, fires in Lantana-invaded areas tend to be tall, reaching the height of the tree canopy. Fires in such areas generally result in a high level of tree attrition. Putting out such fires is very difficult and risky for the forest staff involved.

---

6 Refer Annexure 5 for citation details
7 Refer Annexure 5 for citation details
8 Refer Annexure 5 for citation details

h. Reduction in foraging biomass in large forest areas occupied by Lantana increases the incidence of crop raids in nearby villages by wild animals, thus increasing human-wildlife conflict.

CHAPTER 2

# MANAGEMENT OF *LANTANA CAMARA* – AN OVERVIEW

Management of *Lantana camara* involves three important phases i.e. removal, restoration and maintenance. All these phases are equally important for effective restoration of the invaded areas. This is an important aspect to be borne in mind, as generally most Lantana management initiatives focus only on its removal.

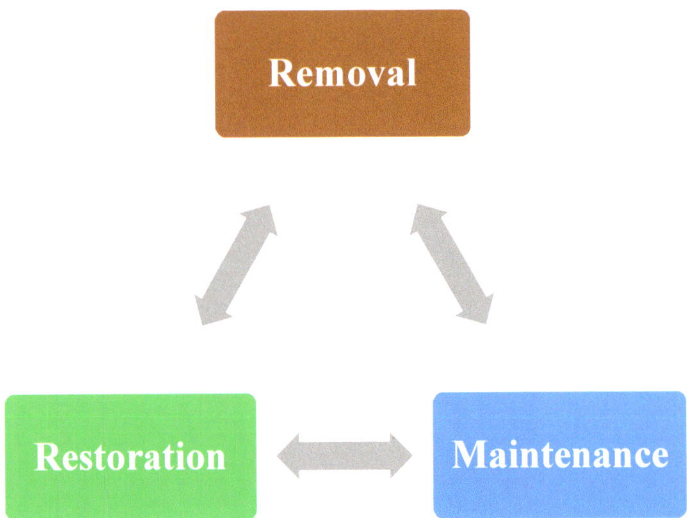


## 2.1 REMOVAL

The removal phase involves the activity of removing Lantana using scientifically proven methods that minimise re-emergence of the plant and at the same time cause minimal collateral damage to the ecosystem. Removal also involves important decisions regarding landscape-level planning, site selection, resources and training, dealing with the removed biomass, etc.

## 2.2 RESTORATION

The restoration phase involves activities that facilitate the recovery of biodiversity in the Lantana-cleared areas. Restoration efforts are needed for at least 3-4 years succeeding the initial year of removal until the site reaches a reasonable degree of biodiversity, self-sustenance and resilience. Hence the restoration activity is of greater importance in the management of Lantana. The restoration phase also involves the removal of re-emerging Lantana and secondary invasive species for 3-4 years succeeding the initial year of removal.

## 2.3 MAINTENANCE

Maintenance refers to the ongoing maintenance of the site after the completion of the restoration phase. This is crucial in sustaining the benefits of the preceding activities and ensuring that the site reaches the highest level of ecological recovery possible. The duration of the maintenance phase is site-dependent based on factors like proximate threats, level of recovery at the end of the restoration phase, potential for ongoing re-invasion, etc. Normally, ongoing maintenance at a minimally resource-intensive level is recommended for 2-3 years.

*"Ecological restoration is the process of assisting the recovery of an ecosystem that has been degraded, damaged or destroyed"*

*- Society for Ecological Restoration*

## CHAPTER 3

# REMOVAL OF *LANTANA CAMARA*

## 3.1 GOVERNING PRINCIPLE FOR THE REMOVAL OF INVASIVE SPECIES

The governing principle for the removal of any invasive plant species is to use scientifically proven methods that minimise re-emergence of the plant and at the same time cause minimal collateral damage to the ecosystem.

## 3.2 CUT-ROOTSTOCK METHOD OF REMOVAL

Detailed studies on the morphology, anatomy and ecology of *Lantana camara* carried out at the Centre of Excellence program of the Ministry of Environment, Forest and Climate Change (MOEF & CC) at the Centre for Environmental Monitoring of Degraded Ecosystems (CEMDE), University of Delhi, led to the development of the successful and easy-to-implement 'Cut-rootstock method' for removal of the weed[9]. This method involves cutting the main tap root of the plant beneath the 'coppicing zone' (transition zone between stem base and rootstock) (refer to Figures 6 and 7). The main rootstock of the Lantana plant is cut 4–6 cm below the soil surface, just below the point where the lateral roots emerge, by hitting the rootstock a few times using a simple manual Gudli or Kudaal (refer to Figures 8 and 9). This method has been used successfully in many protected areas of India like Corbett Tiger Reserve, Rajaji National Park, Sasan Gir National Park, Bandipur National Park, etc.

9 Refer Annexure 5 for citation details

Figure 6 (left): Coppicing zone (yellow arrow) which is the 3-5 cm portion below the soil surface. Cutting zone (red arrow) which is just below the point where lateral roots emerge.

Figure 7 (right): Rootstock after cutting. (Images courtesy: Amit Love, Suresh Babu and C. R. Babu . Management of Lantana, an invasive alien weed, in forest ecosystems of India. Current Science, Vol. 97, no. 10, 25 November 2009)

The hand-held tool can be made by local iron smiths using metal from old and discarded lorry springs. It is around 1.25 kg in weight and has a slight curve as can be seen from the lateral view in Figure 9.

Figures 8 and 9: Images of Kudaal or Gudli used – front and lateral view

The lateral roots can be severed at the base of the plant using the same Gudli or Kudaal. Since Lantana does not produce root suckers, these lateral roots need not be completely removed. Branches of the plant should not be slashed to gain access to the base of the clump during the cut-rootstock method, as vegetative regeneration potential from the fallen stem or branch cuttings is high in the presence of moisture. Instead, the plant should be pushed back using a pole to expose the base, making it easier for the rootstock to be cut.

## 3.3 APPLICATION OF THE CUT-ROOTSTOCK METHOD TO DIFFERENT SIZES OF BUSHES

In the case of small bushes, this method can be implemented by one person. Medium-sized individual bushes can be removed by a 2-person team, with one person pushing the bush back using a forked stick to expose the base of the stem, and the second person cutting the rootstock (refer to Figure 10).

Figure 10: Removal of a medium-sized bush by a 2-person team, one person pushes the bush back using a forked stick while the second person cuts the rootstock

In the case of larger and denser bushes forming small clumps, 2–3 individuals work in a group, with two persons pushing the plant backwards using a pole so that the base is exposed, and the third person cutting the rootstock of the individual plants forming the clump (refer to Figure 11).

Figure 11: Removal of a large-sized bush by a 3-person team, two persons push the bush back using a pole while the third person (middle) cuts the rootstock

In the case of dense clumps consisting of multiple tall plants, a team of 4-6 persons may have to work together to simultaneously cut the rootstocks of contiguous individuals and thereby remove the entire clump in one go (refer to Figure 12).

Figure 12: A very large clump removed using this method. One such cluster when removed clears almost 400-500 sft of space

## 3.4 DEMO VIDEOS OF THE CUT-ROOTSTOCK METHOD OF *LANTANA CAMARA* REMOVAL

The demonstration of the Cut-rootstock method for small, medium and large *Lantana camara* bushes is shown in 3 videos produced by Junglescapes Charitable Trust and can accessed through the following links. The time taken for removal can also be observed from the timer on the videos. It can be seen that the time taken is much shorter than what it would take to slash several branches or uproot the entire root system of the plant (a method used in some forest areas).

**Removal of small, individual *Lantana camara* bushes**

https://www.youtube.com/watch?v=IreVOijPkDE

**Removal of medium-sized, individual *Lantana camara* bushes**

https://www.youtube.com/watch?v=fYuQGN_rxdA

**Removal of large *Lantana camara* clumps consisting of multiple inter-twined bushes**

https://www.youtube.com/watch?v=FK0Mb47F0cE

These videos can also be accessed using the below QR code.

## 3.5 HANDLING OF REMOVED *LANTANA CAMARA* BUSHES

Post removal, the *Lantana camara* bushes are placed upside down (refer to Figure 13) to prevent the root portion from coming into contact with the soil and re-establishing. This also helps supervision as the visible upturned rootstocks indicate the correct use of the Cut-rootstock method. About 6-10 bushes can be collected as a heap in one corner to free up space. Placing the heaps around 15-20 metres apart is important to avoid the risk of spread of forest fires (refer to Figure 14).

These heaps can ideally be left to decompose in the area. The heaps normally reduce in volume and height quickly and fully decompose in 12-15 months. Attempts to clear them from the site can result in collateral damage to pre-existing native vegetation on the plot due to the movement of men and vehicles involved in such clearance. Clearance of heaps is also manpower-intensive and expensive.

*In situ* burning of these bushes needs to be avoided as this will result in the re-emergence of Lantana as the heat generated leads to the breaking of dormancy of sub-soil seed banks. (Refer to Para 3.9). Burning also destroys native seedlings lying underneath, and can also lead to higher secondary invasions.

Figure 13: Removed *Lantana camara* bushes kept upside down with the severed rootstock clearly visible for monitoring

Figure 14: Removed *Lantana camara* bushes kept upside down in heaps that are 25-30 feet apart

## 3.6 ECOLOGICAL USES OF REMOVED *LANTANA CAMARA* BUSHES

Removed bushes lying close to roads can be taken out easily and can be converted into biochar which can, in turn, be used to enrich the soil in the restoration plots. This activity can be carried out by eco-development committees or self-help groups, creating a circular economic model.

Dried Lantana bushes can also be used as bio-fences for native seedlings recruited naturally and for planted saplings to protect them from herbivory. These can also be bundled and placed across small streams to create simple, beaver-like dams to slow down water flow and help improve soil moisture levels[10].

Where feasible, dried Lantana can be given to village hamlets for use as fuelwood for purposes like heating bath water. This can reduce pressure on forests due to fuelwood collection and also help reduce human-wildlife conflict.

## 3.7 ADVANTAGES OF THE CUT-ROOTSTOCK METHOD

The Cut-rootstock method has the following significant advantages:

- The removed plant does not re-emerge or re-coppice.
- Re-emergence of *Lantana camara* from other sources (*in situ* seed bank and seed dispersal from surrounding areas) is observed to be between 20-25% after the first round of removal and around 10% after the second round of removal (refer to Annexure 3 for the Restoration Progression chart). While re-emergence from sub-soil seed banks is normally sporadic, recruitment from seeds dispersed by birds that use tall trees for perching results in denser re-emergence.
- The removal scar on the ground is only 6-8 inches in diameter (refer to Figure 15) and there is very minimal disturbance to the

10 Refer Annexure 5 for citation details

soil. Hence the risk of sub-soil Lantana seeds getting exposed to light and moisture is minimised.

- There is no collateral damage to pre-existing native vegetation. This is critical for aiding the recovery of native vegetation from *in situ* propagules.

This method can be deployed throughout the year, including during dry months, as it does not involve deep digging. Removal during dry summer can be observed in one of the videos cited in para 3.4. In comparison, methods like uprooting the entire root system or mechanical grubbing can be carried out only when soil moisture levels are good.

Figure 15: Typical small scars at *Lantana camara* removed spots with minimal soil disturbance

## 3.8 REPEAT OF REMOVAL OF *LANTANA CAMARA*

Repeated removal of *Lantana camara* is needed for at least 3-4 years after the first year. Particular attention is required under "bird-perching trees" where re-emergence tends to be higher due to dispersal by birds bringing seeds from other areas.

The re-emergence comes down with the emergence of native grasses and shrubs. But it seldom reaches a zero level, with sporadic bushes emerging even after some years through seed dispersal from nearby areas. “Perch trees” continue to remain centres of re-emergence until the total restoration area exceeds the home range of dispersing birds, which is estimated at 1–1.5 km. However, progression in native vegetation tends to exercise biological control over re-emergence to a large extent and is the most sustainable long-term solution (refer to Annexure 3 for the Restoration Progression chart).

## 3.9 REMOVAL METHODS TO BE AVOIDED

The following removal and control methods have significant adverse consequences and therefore not recommended:

a. **Slashing/chopping:**

This method stimulates the shoot buds from the nodes below the chopped portions of *Lantana camara* branches. This leads to the proliferation of new branches that get interwoven into each other leading to the formation of impenetrable thickets. Also, vegetative regeneration takes place from the stem or branch cuttings deposited on the soil (Layering) in the presence of moisture.

b. **Burning:**

Burning stimulates intense basal coppicing of *Lantana camara* even where the above-ground parts of the plant are fully burnt. Surveys of severely fire-affected areas show that almost 100% of burnt plants exhibit profuse basal coppicing (refer to Figures 16 and 17). Burning also leads to the breaking of dormancy of sub-soil seed banks due to the heat, thereby increasing fresh recruitment of Lantana. An image of a Lantana-invaded area that was impacted by a forest fire taken about 18 months after the fire is given in Figure 18.

Burning destroys *in situ* native plant species and causes high collateral damage to diverse fauna. Fire-affected areas are also highly prone to secondary invasions, as well as entry of new invasive species like *Senna spectabilis*.

Figure 16: Intensive basal coppicing of fire-burnt *Lantana camara* bushes

Figure 17: Close-up image of burnt Lantana bush with basal coppicing

Figure 18: Dense Lantana re-invasion after a forest fire

c. **Mechanical or manual grubbing:**

Mechanical grubbing involves removal using machinery like JCBs or similar equipment. Manual grubbing involves digging out the entire root system of the *Lantana camara* bushes. These methods lead to extensive soil disturbance and exposure of dormant, sub-soil Lantana seeds to light. This results in germination and re-establishment of *Lantana camara,* as well as the appearance of secondary weeds. Most areas treated with mechanical grubbing witness an increase in Lantana abundance compared to the pre-removal scenario, making the effort and expenditure infructuous and counter-productive. These methods also result in significant collateral damage to pre-existing native vegetation in the restoration plots.

d. **Chemical and biological methods**

These are not advisable in protected forest areas due to risks or hazards to the native biota and environment.

*"Native plants are the indigenous plant species that have evolved and occur naturally in a particular region, ecosystem, and habitat"*

*- U.S. Forest Service*

# CHAPTER 4

# RESTORATION OF LANTANA-CLEARED AREAS

Restoration of plots where *Lantana camara* has been removed is an extremely important activity. The absence of restoration efforts leads to quick re-invasion of the plots, making the effort and cost involved in removal infructuous. Some key guidelines for the restoration activity are discussed below.

## 4.1 FUNDING AND PREPARATION

Restoration is a long-term activity that takes 3-5 years depending on the intensity of invasion. This is an activity requiring a high degree of planning and preparation in terms of ensuring the availability of native plant propagules, human resources, etc. Adequate budgetary allocation and funding for the full period of restoration is essential for successful restoration.

## 4.2 SETTING RESTORATION GOALS

The objective of restoration is to restore the site closest to its pre-disturbance state, with a **native** floral community composition and structure that is representative of the ecosystem type. This is done by using a relatively undisturbed and healthy site (or sites), of the same ecosystem type and within the same provenance, as a reference model or benchmark. While the ideal restoration goal is to facilitate the revival of 100% of the ecological diversity of the reference model, this may have to be broken down into shorter-term targets such as reaching 50% of the reference in the first 5 years (for more information on developing a reference model please refer to the *International Principles and Standards for the Practice of Ecological Restoration* published by the Society for Ecological Restoration[11]).

11 Refer Annexure 5 for citation details

## 4.3 REVIVING GRASS COVER

Getting native grass cover back is the first line of defence against the re-emergence of *Lantana camara*. Grasses provide multiple benefits for restoration:

a. Grasses help quickly cover areas opened up by *Lantana camara* removal and thereby minimise opportunities for re-emergence of Lantana.
b. Grasses help alleviate the soil degradation caused by the weed.
c. Grasses help improve soil moisture.
d. Grasses are good "nurturing species" that facilitate the establishment of native seedlings between the grass clumps, protecting them from herbivory in the early stages of their growth.

Grasses can be propagated by assisting natural regeneration or by the introduction of propagules, as discussed below.

- In low and medium invasion plots with pre-existing patches of grass between *Lantana camara* bushes (refer to Figure 19), these grasses tend to spread naturally once Lantana is removed. The spread of grasses may also be accelerated by simple methods to augment soil moisture, like short and shallow trenches on hill slopes or swales on flat lands (refer to Figures 20 and 21). These are temporary structures that get filled with soil naturally within a year but help significantly in augmenting moisture.

Figure 19: Grassy patches between Lantana bushes in low and medium-density plots

Figure 20: A 4-feet long shallow trench made on a barren hill slope. These trenches are around 9 inches deep and are low-cost but effective.

Figure 21: A typical swale which is a shallow saucer-shaped structure ideal for facilitating grass regeneration naturally, or through seed dibbling

- Sites with barren patches will need the introduction of grass propagules either through seed dibbling or through the planting of grass slips. This is normally true in the case of areas with a higher density of *Lantana camara*. Management of Lantana in such sites will therefore need a higher level of preparatory work in the form of the collection of propagules of grasses and other native plants. It is advisable to remove Lantana only after such preparatory work is done to avoid re-invasion and secondary invasions.
- Many grass species do not spread to or establish well in semi-shaded areas under trees. Shade-loving grass species have to be selected for propagation under trees.
- It is important to identify the grass species native to the ecosystem and arrange for the collection of grass seeds during the seed-bearing season.
- Seed dibbling is successful for less-palatable / awned grass species like *Heteropogon contortus* as these face lower grazing pressure from herbivores. In the case of more palatable and softer grass species, seed dibbling tends to be less successful

as the young and succulent shoots are heavily browsed. Transplanting slips using mature source clumps is more successful for such grasses. The higher silica content in these mature slips reduces the risk of herbivory.

- Refer to Figures 22-25 on the process of transplanting of grass slips.

Figure 22: Grass clumps collected

Figure 23: Individual slips separated from the clump

Figure 24: Transplanting of slips

Figure 25: Establishment of slips after transplanting

## 4.4 REVIVING 'BLOCK' SPECIES

'Block species' are native plant species that help provide an effective biological defence against the re-emergence of *Lantana camara*. These species achieve this by quickly occupying the space vacated by Lantana and crowding or shading out fresh Lantana.

- Many grass, shrub and herb species are excellent block species as they establish quickly after the removal of Lantana.
- Many shrub species are observed to be recruited naturally in good numbers in *Lantana camara*-removed areas. This phenomenon of hyper-recruitment of native species post-removal of invasive species results from the freeing-up of space and natural resources[12].
- We have observed that native plant species like *Dendrocalamus strictus, Zizyphus oenoplia, Dodonaea viscosa, Grewia villosa, Barleria buxifolia, Argyreia cuneata, Tarenna asiatica, Maytenus emarginata, Acacia pennata* and *Capparis zeylanica* act as good block species in our restoration plots.
- Seasonal herbs also occur naturally in good abundance in *Lantana camara*-cleared areas and are observed to compete effectively with Lantana and secondary invasive species like Parthenium.
- Fast-growing pioneer tree species can also serve as block species as they help build a canopy that shades out Lantana.

Identifying the 'block' species specific to the habitat and planning for their propagation (where their natural recruitment is low) through seeds, saplings or stem cuttings is recommended.

## 4.5 REVIVING PIONEER PLANT SPECIES

Pioneer plant species are those that are capable of establishing and growing in the degraded conditions present in sites where Lantana has been removed recently.

12 Refer Annexure 5 for citation details

Pioneer plant species play an important role in the restoration process. These provide a number of ecosystem services that have a key role in the ecosystem's recovery process.

a. Pioneer species help in reversing soil erosion.
b. Pioneer species help in improving multiple soil parameters e.g. soil moisture content, soil nutrient levels, soil organic content, etc.
c. Pioneer species help in creating the right environment for successional species to establish. Hence it is advisable to initially focus on these species before planning for the revival of successional species.

It is important to identify key pioneer tree and shrub species native to the restoration site and plan for their revival.

## 4.6 LEVERAGING ON NATURAL REGENERATION POTENTIAL

Our experience shows that many plots with low and medium-density *Lantana camara* have good potential for recovery of native plant species through natural regeneration. This is facilitated by pre-existing native vegetation, sub-soil seed banks or root fragments and seed migration from nearby areas.

Even plots with a higher density of invasion witness the recovery of many native species (particularly of pioneer and early successional species) naturally. This is a result of the freeing-up of space and natural resources, which in turn attracts seed migration towards these plots.

Assisting or accelerating natural regeneration is called the "Assisted Natural Regeneration" (ANR) approach. This involves efforts to remove barriers to natural regeneration e.g. measures for harvesting rainwater, reversing soil erosion, improving soil health, reducing anthropogenic pressures, etc.

Some ANR interventions that have been effective in our restoration efforts are short 4-feet long shallow trenches (refer to Figure 20 on page 48), shallow swales (refer to Figure 21 on page 49), rock detention structures (RDS) across small streams that slow down water flow (refer to Figure 26), etc. These are temporary structures that get filled up by soil in a period of 12-18 months, but during this period augment soil moisture significantly.

Figure 26: A typical Rock Detention Structure or Stone Overflow made with loose stones that slows down water flow and improves moisture availability

Natural juvenile support is another effective ANR intervention. This involves making a short shallow trench near a naturally recruited juvenile plant (refer to Figure 27). This method helps accelerate the establishment and growth of the juvenile plant and is very helpful in the case of tree species.

Figure 27: Short and shallow trench to augment moisture for a naturally recruited juvenile plant indicated by the yellow arrow

ANR has several advantages as discussed below.

a. ANR is a low-cost restoration approach, with costs being 60-70% lower than a sapling-planting approach. This allows the restoration of a much larger area with the same amount of resources. ANR has the potential to be a key enabler for landscape level restoration projects.
b. ANR allows natural organisation without the disturbance of ecological niches.
c. Naturally recruited plants generally have a higher degree of resilience and survival rates as compared to introduced saplings.
d. Recovery of vegetation attracts pollinators to the restoration plots, which helps accelerate the restoration process.

e. Recovering vegetation also attracts herbivores and other seed-dispersing fauna like elephants, sloth bears and jungle fowl to the plots. Rewilding by diverse native species of fauna facilitates the dispersal of seeds of diverse native plant species. Long-distance seed dispersal by bigger fauna like elephants often helps the revival of multiple plant species.

A good restoration strategy is to observe the natural recruitment at a site for 18-24 months to assess species coming up through an ANR approach and identify the species gaps for introduction through seeds or saplings.

Images of plots that have recovered primarily through the Assisted Natural Regeneration approach are given in Figures 28-30.

Figure 28: Naturally recovering grassland after Lantana removal

Figure 29: Naturally recovering mixed forest after Lantana removal

Figure 30: Natural recovery in fire-affected area after removal of Lantana

## 4.7 SEED COLLECTION, PROCESSING, STORAGE AND PRE-TREATMENT

The collection, processing and storage of seeds of native plant species forms an important part of the restoration process. In particular, seeds of rarer tree and shrub species are normally not available from external sources and have to be collected locally. Guidelines for seed collection and storage are as follows:

a. Collection of seeds from the local provenance is recommended to ensure their genetic integrity.
b. Collection from multiple, spatially separated individuals of each species is also recommended for greater resilience.
c. A seed collection calendar is recommended to ensure seeds of plants with different phenology are collected.
d. Different seeds have different viability periods, after which the viability starts declining. It is ideal to use the seeds within their viability period for maximising germination rates.
e. Protocols for seed cleaning, storage and handling are also important for maximising the productivity of the seeds.
f. Protocols for the pre-treatment of seeds are also important. The pre-treatment generally varies according to the hardness of the seed coat.

Some reference books on native trees (e.g. Common Dryland Trees of Karnataka[13]) as well as some online herbariums provide information on the phenology and pre-treatment methods for different species of native seeds.

## 4.8 SEED PROCUREMENT

Seed procurement may be required in some situations where seeds are not available locally. Care has to be taken to procure seeds only from very reliable sources to avoid seed contamination. Contaminated seeds are often a major source of introduction of invasive as well as exotic plant species. Accredited seed suppliers provide information on the locations from where the seeds have been harvested, the timeline of harvesting, germination rates under test conditions, etc. which is useful for procurement decision-making.

13 Refer Annexure 5 for citation details

## 4.9 SEED DIBBLING

Seed dibbling involves making a small hole in the soil, dropping the seed and covering the same with soil. The size of the hole is generally twice the size of the seed. In the case of some plant species with smaller seeds, more than one seed may be dibbled in a hole. Seed dibbling has the following advantages:

a. It is a lower-cost option as compared to sapling planting and therefore makes it possible to restore larger areas with the same amount of funds.
b. Seedlings germinating *in situ* from dibbled seeds are generally more resilient and able to establish better (refer to Figures 31-34).
c. Planted saplings tend to face high browsing as well as trampling pressure from animals and therefore survival rates tend to be lower compared to seedlings recruited *in situ*.

It is important to dibble the right seed in the right place. This depends on factors like the moisture requirements of the plant species, the soil and sunlight conditions that are most suitable for the species to establish and grow, etc. These principles apply to sapling planting as well.

Figure 31: *Bambusa bambos* (left) and Figure 32: *Heteropogon contortus* (right) - germinating from seed dibbling

Figure 33: Eluchi (*Z.mauritiana*) seeds collected (left) and Figure 34: same germinating after dibbling (right)

## 4.10 SAPLING PLANTING

Sapling planting in open forest areas faces many challenges e.g. herbivory, trampling, stress and difficulty in establishing in a new environment, uncertain rainfall patterns, etc. As a result, survival rates tend to be low. Protection against browsing by measures like solar fences is generally not viable in large forest landscapes. Even where fencing has been attempted, these are often breached by animals.

Intensive sapling planting also has the risk of suppressing *in situ* propagules of native plants. However, sapling planting may be successful in areas with higher rainfall levels and lower herbivore pressures. Also, some plant species tend to establish better through the sapling planting route.

The cost-benefits of this method may have to be evaluated on a case-to-case basis based on site conditions.

CHAPTER 5

# PLANNING OF RESTORATION SITES AND PLOTS

The proper planning of areas to be taken up for restoration is crucial for the success of the efforts as this enables maximising the ecological benefits within the shortest possible time and with the least resources. Guidelines for the planning of sites and plots are discussed below.

## 5.1 GUIDELINES FOR CLASSIFICATION OF *LANTANA CAMARA* DENSITY

The density of invasion plays a key role in decision-making on site and plot selection. *Lantana camara* can be classified into 4 categories based on the density of invasion, namely Low, Medium, High and Impenetrable. The below characteristics of different densities of invasion can be used as guidance for classification and site selection:

a. Low-density plots have individual *Lantana camara* bushes with a height of 4-6 feet, with the weed covering 20-30% of the forest floor (refer to Figure 35). Such plots are typically found in low-moisture retention areas like hill slopes, areas with higher canopy cover and areas with rocky soil substrate. Areas in the early stages of invasion also have low densities.

Figure 35: Typical plot with low-density Lantana invasion

b. Medium-density plots have either individual *Lantana camara* bushes or small clumps of 2-3 individuals, with a height of 6-8 feet (refer to Figure 36). Lantana is observed to cover 30-50% of the forest floor. Medium-density plots typically have higher moisture retention and are areas that are relatively flatter or with gentle gradients.

Figure 36: Typical plot with medium-density Lantana invasion

- As can be observed from Figures 35 and 36, both low and medium-density plots have grassy patches in between the *Lantana camara* bushes.
- Low-density plots also generally have good native plant abundance between and under the *Lantana camara* bushes. Medium-density plots have native vegetation to a lesser degree but still have a reasonably good presence of grasses.

c. High-density invasion is characterised by large clumps of 5-8 individuals per clump and canopy heights of 9-15 feet. *Lantana camara* is observed to cover 60-80% of the forest floor (refer to Figure 37). Native vegetation in-between Lantana bushes is significantly lower although not totally absent. This profile is generally seen in areas with higher soil moisture levels e.g. valleys, banks of streams and rivers, higher rainfall regions, areas with rich loamy soil, low-lying lands, etc.

Figure 37: Typical plot with high-density Lantana invasion

d. Impenetrable *Lantana camara* is where the plant appears as very dense and intertwined clusters of 10-20 individuals, forming an impenetrable thicket that even large mammals find difficult to pass through. Lantana is observed to cover almost 100% of the forest floor (refer to Figure 38). These clusters can grow to a height of 15-20 feet and are often seen clinging to tall trees or bamboo clumps. In general, there is no native vegetation observed under such impenetrable patches. Impenetrable Lantana is normally formed in areas that have witnessed high disturbances e.g. forest fires, use of heavy machinery like JCBs to remove Lantana, etc.

Figure 38: Typical plot with impenetrable thickets of Lantana

## 5.2 PLAN REMOVAL AND RESTORATION IN PLOTS WITH EARLIER STAGES OF INVASION

As per globally recognised principles for the management of invasive plant species, removal and restoration should be planned first in areas with lower densities of invasion before taking up areas with higher densities of invasion. IUCN Guidelines recommend that priority be given to sites where a new alien invasion has occurred and is not yet well established[14].

The benefits of this approach are as below:

a. This approach gives a good opportunity to tackle the invasion in its early or mid-early stages, thereby preventing its progression to a high-density invasion. This helps minimise the build-up of propagules of invasive species.

14 Refer Annexure 5 for citation details

b. Such plots have good pre-existing native vegetation which tends to occupy the cleared areas quickly, reducing the effort required to restore the plots. In the case of high-density *Lantana camara*, there is hardly any native vegetation in the plots and the soil is also highly degraded. Therefore restoration efforts tend to be far more intensive requiring a high degree of preparation. These plots often tend to face higher levels of invasion by secondary invasives.
c. The cost of restoring such plots is significantly lower compared to high-density plots. Therefore it is possible to restore biodiversity and healthy wildlife habitats over a much larger area with the same amount of funding.
d. This approach enables quick recovery of native vegetation over a larger area. This in turn can serve as a nucleus of native plant propagules that facilitate recovery in nearby areas. This is similar to the principle of 'applied nucleation'[15].
e. These plots also help the restoration teams gain field experience and knowledge in managing *Lantana camara*.

However, most invaded sites are likely to have a mix of low, medium and high-density invasion, and not addressing all of them together would raise a high risk of re-invasion. Hence, sites where low and medium-density invasion plots constitute at least 75-80% of the total area may be selected.

## 5.3 PLAN CONTIGUOUS PLOTS TO MAXIMISE RESTORATION BENEFITS

Planning of contiguous plots helps create a larger restored area as compared to plots that are dispersed and disconnected from each other. Contiguous plots help minimise the risk of re-invasion from adjacent plots. They also help progressively increase the abundance of native vegetation creating a multiplier effect. Refer to Figure 39 for

15 Refer Annexure 5 for citation details

an example of contiguous plot planning of 15 plots totalling around 375 Ha.

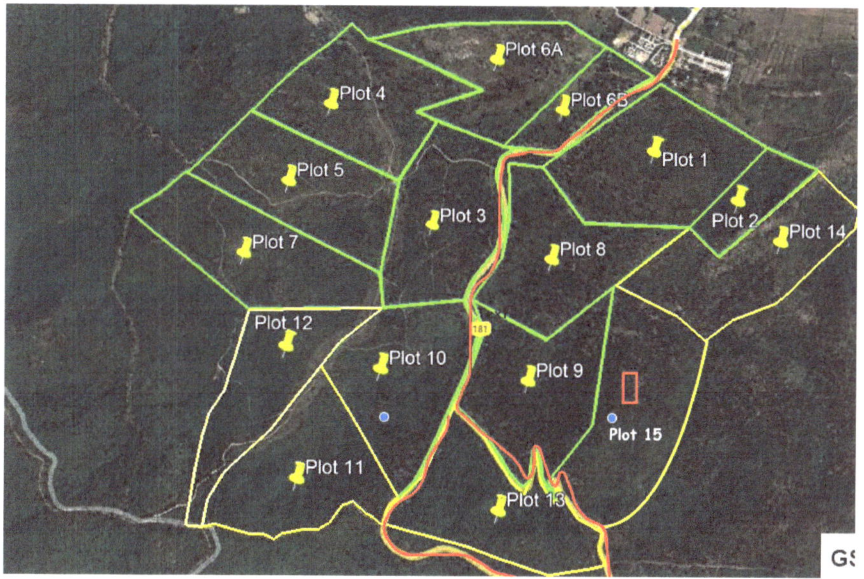


Figure 39: Example of 15 contiguous plots totalling 375 Ha

## 5.4 OTHER IMPORTANT CONSIDERATIONS IN SITE AND PLOT PLANNING

Other important considerations in site selection are as below:

a. Select sites with natural advantages like sites adjacent to uninvaded and healthy areas to quickly expand the Lantana-free area.

b. In the case of hill slopes start invasive removal at the highest point and work downwards to prevent Lantana seeds from migrating downhill during monsoons.

c. As far as possible, start with areas with the least presence of secondary invasive species like Parthenium and Eupatorium, either inside the plot or in nearby areas.

d. **In case of the presence of *Senna spectabilis* on the restoration plot or in nearby areas, care should be taken to ensure that these are removed simultaneously along with *Lantana camara*. This is because *Senna spectabilis* has been observed to occupy Lantana-removed areas rapidly.**

e. An individual plot size of not more than 20-25 Ha is recommended for effective plot supervision and management.

## 5.5 IMPORTANCE OF A LANDSCAPE-LEVEL APPROACH

The management of *Lantana camara* requires a landscape-level approach. This involves taking up a large and contiguous area at each site for restoration. A minimum scale of 400-500 Ha (1000 acres and above) at a single site is recommended. Removal activities carried out on smaller sites are generally not effective as these tend to get re-invaded quickly by propagules of invasive plants from surrounding areas. An exception to this principle is areas with isolated fresh invasions where removal should be planned immediately before further spread.

## 5.6 GRID-BASED RESTORATION METHODOLOGY

The objective of the grid-based methodology is to facilitate more effective implementation and supervision of the restoration activities. For example, a 25 Ha plot can be divided into 4-5 grids of around 6-7 Ha each to facilitate closer monitoring and supervision. This is advisable since supervising a large 25 Ha plot as one block is difficult. The number and size of grids will have to be decided based on the size of the plot and site parameters.

The grids are marked based on topographic features and the relative presence of invasive species so that there is reasonable homogeneity of restoration parameters within each grid. Given in Figure 40 is an example of 5 grids marked in a plot of 25 Ha. In this plot, the grids 1 and

2 are on a hill slope with an elevation of approximately 1045 metres. These grids have medium *Lantana camara* density. Grids 3 and 4 are relatively on level land with an elevation of about 930 metres and have higher density of *Lantana camara*. Grid 5 has been marked separately due to a high presence of *Senna spectabilis*.

Figure 40: Marking of 5 grids in a plot of 25 Ha

## 5.7 PLANNING OF RESTORATION TEAMS

The time taken for a 10-person, well-trained team to remove Lantana over an area of one acre is estimated as below:

a. Low-density invasion: 1 to 1.5 days
b. Medium-density invasion: 2 to 2.5 days
c. High-density invasion: 3 to 4 days

With 5 teams, Lantana can be removed in a plot of around 50-60 acres (20-25 hectares) having medium density Lantana in a month. A team size of 10 to 12 persons is normally ideal from the point of view of efficiency and ease of supervision. However, more than one team may have to be deployed at a site based on the scale involved.

The above are broad estimates and the time taken may vary with factors like weather conditions, experience of the team, working hours, etc. It is recommended that a closer assessment of time taken by different teams is made at the initial stages of the project to help better planning.

CHAPTER 6

# PROTOCOLS FOR RESTORATION ACTIVITIES

The restoration of Lantana-invaded plots is a complex exercise involving a number of activities. Following standard process protocols is important to ensure the effectiveness of restoration as well as to ensure consistency in implementation across plots and sites.

## 6.1 RESTORATION PROCESS FLOW CHART

A process flow chart showing the normal sequence of activities is given in Annexure 1 and can be used as a reference. A brief description of the activities mentioned in the flow chart is given below:

a. **Plot and grid marking**

Plots are normally planned using Google Earth after conducting a preliminary reconnaissance of the site. Subsequently, the plots are physically marked on the ground using the GPS coordinates in the Google Earth map. Plot markers used in the field to mark the boundaries may be of different types e.g. stone piles, flags, significant landmarks like large trees or rocks, etc.

b. **Baseline plot surveys and photos**

- Baseline surveys of the plot are carried out prior to the start of the removal activity to gain a good understanding of the plot. These surveys cover a number of aspects like the physical features of the plot, density and spread of invasive species, soil and hydrological conditions, presence of roads or other intrusions, anthropogenic pressures, etc.
- Baseline surveys of native flora are also required to be carried out. These are ideally carried out immediately after the removal of *Lantana camara* to facilitate easier identification of smaller plants.
- Baseline photographs depicting the pre-removal status of the plots are also important.

c. **Restoration planning**

The information gathered through the baseline plot surveys is used to draw up the restoration plan. Apart from the removal of invasive species, the plan covers details of post-removal restoration activities to be carried out. An example of a baseline survey-cum-restoration plan document is given in Annexure 4.

d. **Lantana camara removal**

This involves the activity of removal of *Lantana camara* and other invasive species observed on the plot. Removal is normally carried out in sequential strips of around 20-25 feet width each covering the length of the plot, and hence called the "strip method". Figure 41 gives an example of the strip method.

e. **Combing**

This is an important activity post removal. Combing involves supervisory staff carrying out a thorough inspection of each plot/ grid to ensure that all *Lantana camara* (and other invasive) plants have been removed. The supervisory staff is normally accompanied by 2-3 persons carrying Gudlis or Kudaals so that weedy plants that have been missed to be removed earlier can be removed during the combing.

f. **Post-removal restoration**

This activity has been discussed in Chapter 4.

g. **Monitoring and documenting the recovery of native flora**

This activity is discussed in detail in Chapter 7.

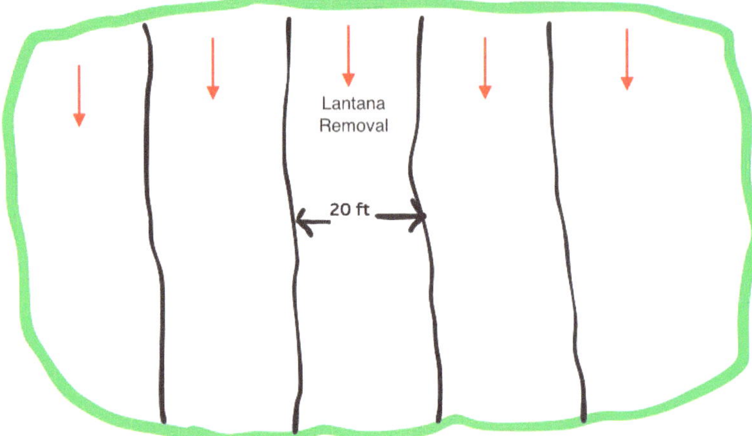


Figure 41: Strip method of removal with strips of around 20 feet width

## 6.2 ANNUAL RESTORATION CALENDAR

Ecological restoration of *Lantana camara* invaded plots involves activities that need to be implemented during the entire year. This requires an annual restoration calendar to be prepared to facilitate planning. An example of a restoration calendar is given in Annexure 2.

CHAPTER 7

# MONITORING OF RESTORATION PLOTS

## 7.1 MONITORING THE RE-EMERGENCE OF INVASIVE ALIEN SPECIES

Re-invasion by *Lantana camara* from sub-soil seed banks as well as through seed dispersal from nearby areas normally persists for 3-4 years. In particular, re-invasion is higher below large trees used by birds for perching (called 'perch trees'). Hence monitoring of re-emergence once in 6 months is essential for facilitating timely removal. The intensity of re-invasion tends to progressively reduce with the emergence of native grasses and other native vegetation.

Secondary invasive like *Chromolaena odorata* and *Parthenium hysterophorus* pose a threat in *Lantana camara* removed areas. The occurrence of secondary invasive species is generally higher in plots alongside forest roads and lower in areas without roads. Hence monitoring of secondary invasions becomes important to enable early removal.

The presence of both primary and secondary invasives decreases with the increase in the density of native vegetation, mainly block species of grasses and shrubs. It is therefore important to monitor the revival of native vegetation at regular intervals.

Annexure 3 gives the typical restoration progression of a site over 4-5 years of restoration effort.

## 7.2 MONITORING THE REVIVAL OF NATIVE VEGETATION

Monitoring of the revival of native vegetation helps gain important feedback on the status of the restoration efforts. Monitoring is normally done through vegetation surveys carried out using sampling quadrats. The survey results are compared with the baseline surveys carried out at the start of the project to measure progression.

A typical sampling quadrat layout in a 25 Ha plot is given in Figure 42. This consists of 24 quadrats of 10x10 m each. This provides a sample size of around 1% of the plot area. Quadrats are placed randomly to avoid bias, but at the same time distributed across the plot in a manner that varied ecological conditions present on the plot are represented adequately.

Some practitioners use the line transect methodology for vegetation surveys. This is also an effective method provided the transects are planned in a way to be representative of the plot.

Vegetation surveys are recommended once in 6-12 months depending on the resources available.

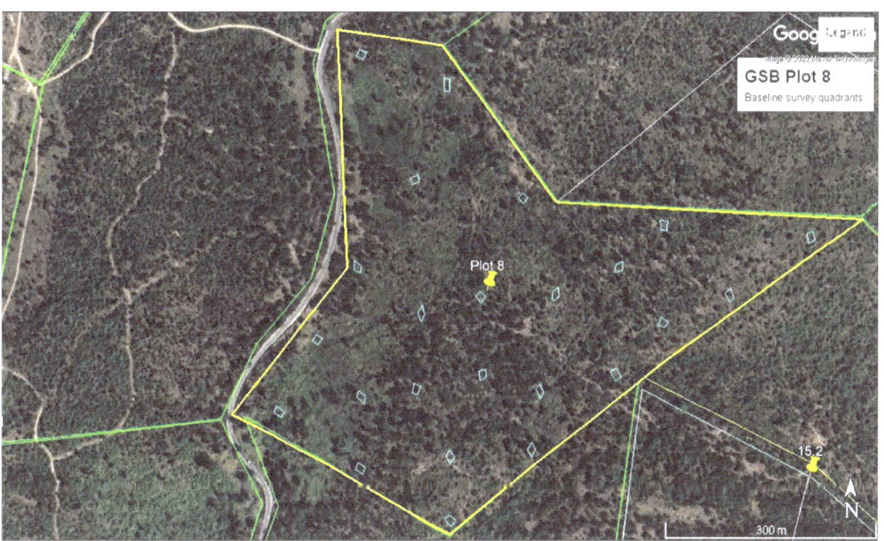


Figure 42: Positioning of 24 survey quadrants in a 25 Ha plot

## 7.3 PARAMETERS TO BE INCLUDED IN VEGETATION SURVEYS

Below are some of the parameters or metrics that may be included while designing a plan for vegetation surveys.

- Species diversity with classification by plant habit. This gives an indication of species and structural diversity.

- Frequency of occurrence or abundance of species. This can be done using a DAFOR classification scale (i.e. Dominant, Abundant, Frequent, Occasional and Rare) or by using a simpler FOR scale (Frequent, Occasional and Rare).
- Distribution between adult and juvenile plants. This gives an idea of the recruitment and succession levels.
- Distribution between pioneer and successional species.
- Distribution between perennial and annual species.
- Distribution between browsed, partially browsed and non-browsed species to gauge the potential for rewilding by herbivores.
- Presence of rare, endemic and threatened species.
- Any other parameter that is contextually relevant.

## 7.4 TIME-LAPSE PHOTOGRAPHS

Time-lapse photographs are images of specific locations in the restoration plot captured at periodic intervals. These give a visual representation of the progression of the restoration project. These images normally have highlights like prominent hills or trees that serve as markers to ensure each image is of the same location. Refer to images 43-46 for examples of time-lapse photographs of an area where Lantana has been removed. These images may be captured along with the recording of associated GPS coordinates to ensure the integrity of documentation.

Figure 43: Plot covered entirely with Lantana prior to removal.
Hills in the background are used as a marker for time-lapse images.

Figure 44: Same plot post-removal and restoration.
Time-lapse image captured after 24 months.

Figure 45: Plot covered entirely with Lantana prior to removal. Hills in the background are used as a marker for time-lapse images.

Figure 46: Same plot post-removal and restoration. Time-lapse image captured after 24 months.

## 7.5 MONITORING REWILDING BY FAUNAL SPECIES

Rewilding by native faunal species is an important proxy indicator of the status of revival of the habitat and its functional attributes. This can be monitored through visual evidence collected during line transects e.g. direct sightings, scat or droppings, pug or hoof marks, nests, carcasses or remains of prey animals, etc. Camera traps can be deployed where feasible.

The presence of keystone or flagship species of fauna provides reassurance on the recovery of broader habitat attributes. However, as these species are generally adaptable to degradation, their presence may not provide feedback on the degree of recovery of ecological niches. Surveys of taxa that are more sensitive to habitat degradation, like insects and birds, are also recommended as these can provide information on the revival of ecological niches.

*"Restoration projects are unlikely to succeed if the sites are not revisited after the completion of initial restoration activities"*

*- UN Decade on Ecosystem Restoration (2021-30)*

CHAPTER 8

# MAINTENANCE OF RESTORATION PLOTS

Post the completion of the restoration efforts, the restoration plots need to be maintained for the subsequent 3-4 years to ensure that the benefits of restoration are sustained. While maintenance is not a resource or finance-intensive activity, it is crucial and yields significant benefits over the long term.

## 8.1 TYPES OF MAINTENANCE ACTIVITIES

Maintenance normally includes the following activities:

a. Carry out periodic combing of plots to detect any sporadic re-emergence of *Lantana camara* and carry out removal.
b. Detect the presence of secondary invasive species and take immediate action for eradication.
c. Monitor native vegetation progression to assess if the recovery process is moving towards the reference model.
d. Identify other threats and plan mitigative actions e.g. new linear intrusions like roads, livestock grazing, etc.
e. Plan other actions to secure the benefits of restoration e.g. safeguarding habitat linkages, facilitating the establishment of rare or endangered plant species, managing anthropogenic pressures, etc.

## 8.2 PLANNING OF MAINTENANCE ACTIVITIES

The maintenance phase of the project has to be planned well in advance as part of the overall project plan. Also, adequate funding has to be allocated for this phase. Without planning and funding, maintenance activities get overlooked in many projects.

Planning also includes assigning responsibilities for maintenance activities. These could be assigned to small caretaker teams or community organisations like eco-development committees or self-help groups.

## 8.3 MANAGEMENT OF SECONDARY INVASIVE SPECIES

Secondary invasive species like *Chromolaena odorata, Parthenium hysterophorus, etc.* are a significant risk in many restoration plots. The risk is higher in plots closer to roads or where adjacent areas have a presence of these species. Some of these secondary weeds are also spread by the seeds attaching themselves to the bodies of fauna.

Early detection of the emergence of secondary invasive species is important. Where observed, these weeds have to be removed immediately. The general principle is to remove these weedy plants prior to their flowering and seeding cycle to avoid the build-up of seed banks. A good understanding of the phenology of these species, in the context of the local climatic conditions, becomes important.

The methodology for removal of secondary invasive species will vary from species to species. Protocols for individual secondary invasive species will therefore have to be formulated wherever needed. It is observed that the abundance of secondary weeds declines gradually with prompt removal and the recovery of native vegetation.

## 8.4 STAKEHOLDER ENGAGEMENT

As per the recommendations in the 'Standards of Practice to Guide Ecosystem Restoration[16] published by UN-FAO, the involvement of local community stakeholders in the maintenance phase of a restoration project is crucial for long-term sustainability. This helps create greater ownership and awareness among successive generations of community members of the importance of maintaining the native biodiversity of the area.

16 Refer Annexure 5 for citation details

*"Indigenous and other traditional peoples have long associations with nature and a deep understanding of it"*

*- International Union for Conservation of Nature*

CHAPTER 9

# CAPACITY BUILDING

As can be observed from the previous chapters, restoration of Lantana-invaded landscapes is a rigorous, long-term and intensive activity. This requires adequate capacity in terms of knowledge, skills and field experience. Building capacity is therefore important to ensure success in these efforts.

## 9.1 FOCUS AREAS FOR CAPACITY-BUILDING

Capacity has to be built in the following areas through appropriate training:

a. Project planning and design
b. Project management
c. Field implementation
d. Field supervision
e. Monitoring and documentation
f. Fundraising
g. Stakeholder engagement

## 9.2 COLLABORATIONS

Ecological restoration is a multi-disciplinary activity and requires knowledge of a wide array of disciplines. It is normally not feasible for any organisation to possess expertise in all of them. Collaborations with subject-matter experts can strengthen projects significantly. Some areas where external expertise may be needed are:

a. Plant identification and field botany
b. Restoration standards and protocols
c. Soil and hydrological sciences
d. Seed collection and handling
e. Nursery management

## 9.3 TRADITIONAL AND INDIGENOUS KNOWLEDGE

Successful ecological restoration requires the integration of scientific and traditional ecological knowledge. Scientific knowledge provides the principles and protocols for restoration. Traditional ecological knowledge (TEK) provides inputs on site conditions and micro-ecological factors that play a key role in implementation.

Junglescapes has been partnering with indigenous community members from around 10 villages surrounding Bandipur National Park. These community members contribute valuable information on aspects which help in understanding the local ecology and the heterogeneity present across the sites and plots. Examples of information available through TEK are as below:

- Soil types in different parts of the site
- Details of watersheds and multiple orders of streams
- Native plant distribution across the site
- Presence and location of adult, seed-bearing trees
- Feeding habits of different herbivores
- Faunal movement patterns
- Rainfall patterns
- Climatic conditions

## 9.4 PARTICIPATION OF LOCAL COMMUNITY MEMBERS

The participation of community members in project implementation is of significance because of the following reasons:

a. As discussed above, they contribute valuable information for project planning.

b. Lantana removal and the subsequent restoration and maintenance activities are mostly human resource-based. Participation of community members with good knowledge of the local terrain and ecology is vital for effective field implementation.

c. Ecological restoration provides sustainable livelihoods for the local communities, creating a win-win relationship between them and the ecology surrounding them.
d. Participation helps create local stewardship for the restoration efforts.

**Junglescapes will be glad to assist in capacity building by conducting training workshops on the management of *Lantana camara*. Interested organisations may please contact us by email at info@junglescapes.org**

CHAPTER 10

# CONCLUSION

*Lantana camara* is one of the oldest invasive plant species in India. As a result, it is well-established in many areas that it has invaded. However, there are still uninvaded and healthy patches within these invaded landscapes. These patches serve as the last remaining reference sites that can be used as benchmarks for restoration. Also, these patches are invaluable sources of propagules of rare plant species. It is therefore extremely important to protect these areas and monitor them closely for any signs of invasion by Lantana and other invasive species. Keeping these areas pristine should be a top priority in the conservation plans of these areas.

A number of initiatives on Lantana focus primarily on its removal. As has been emphasised in many parts of this manual, post-removal restoration is more important than removal.

As Lantana is a well-entrenched species, eradicating it is difficult. There will always be some re-emergence from time to time in restored areas. Maintenance of restored plots therefore is an important activity. Significant biodiversity benefits can be achieved with minimal investment in maintenance.

Apart from the ecological benefits, the restored and structurally diverse habitats can sequester significantly higher amounts of carbon compared to invaded areas. Recent research shows that forests with rewilding by fauna sequester three to four times more carbon than forests with a low abundance of fauna[17]. Restoration facilitates the return of almost all taxa of fauna to restored sites. Hence the carbon sequestration potential of these sites could be much higher.

---

17 Refer Annexure 5 for citation details

While the scale of invasion by Lantana is very large, by using a landscape-level approach we can restore fairly large areas within two decades. This calls for a strategic approach and the adoption of good restoration practices. We hope the information provided in this manual will help practitioners in this regard.

# ANNEXURES

# ANNEXURE 1: RESTORATION PROCESS FLOW CHART

| Phase | Action | Step |
|---|---|---|
| PRE-REMOVAL ACTIVITY | Plot and grid marking | 1 |
| | ↓ | |
| | Baseline surveys and restoration planning | 2 |
| | ↓ | |
| 1st ROUND REMOVAL | *L. camara* removal by Cut-root stock method<br>a. Removal by strip method<br>b. Upturning the removed plants<br>c. Forming heaps for decomposting<br>d. Grid-wise combing | 3 |
| | ↓ | |
| POST-REMOVAL RESTORATION | Soil / hydrology improvement<br>Seed dibbling<br>Sapling planting<br>Grass slip transplantation | 4 |
| | ↓ | |
| | Monitoring / documenting recovery of native flora | 5 |
| | ↓ | |
| 2nd / 3rd ROUND REMOVAL | Repeat steps 3, 4 and 5<br>(Continue for 3-4 years) | 6 |

# ANNEXURE 2: EXAMPLE OF ANNUAL RESTORATION CALENDAR

| S.No | Activity | Jan | Feb | Mar | Apr | May | Jun | Jul | Aug | Sep | Oct | Nov | Dec |
|---|---|---|---|---|---|---|---|---|---|---|---|---|---|
| 1 | Plot and grid marking, baseline surveys | | | | | | | | | | | | |
| 2 | Invasive removal including combing | | | | | | | | | | | | |
| 3 | Hydrological improvement (RDS structures, beaver dams, trenches, swales) | | | | | | | | | | | | |
| 4 | Native plant seed collection, processing, and storage | All habits | | Shrub & Tree species | | | | | | | | | Grasses |
| 5 | Sapling procurement | | | | | | | | | | | | |
| 6 | Seed dibbling | | | | | | | | | | | | |
| 7 | Grass root slip collection and transplantation | | | | | | | | | | | | |
| 8 | Sapling planting | | | | | | | | | | | | |
| 9 | Vegetation surveys | | | | | | | | | | | | |

Note: This is an illustrative example of an annual restoration calendar and may have to be customized to individual project contexts.

# ANNEXURE 3: ECOLOGICAL RESTORATION PROGRESSION CHART FOR IAS INVADED AREAS

| | Year 1 | Year 2 | Year 3 | Years 4-6 |
|---|---|---|---|---|
| Restoration actions | 1st round removal of Lantana / Senna; grass seed dibbling / grass slip transplanting | 2nd round Lantana /Senna/secondary invasive removal; grass & other native species' seed dibbling + natural regeneration | 3rd round Lantana /Senna/secondary invasive removal; grass & other native species' seed dibbling + natural regeneration | Continue monitoring and maintenance |
| Lantana / Senna | ↑ High presence: 60-90% of plot | ↓ Re-emergence: 25-30% | ↓ Re-emergence: 10-15% | ↓ Re-emergence minimal and under good control |
| Grasses | ↓ Very low grass cover of **10-20% of plot; mainly non-palatable species** | ↑ Grass cover spreads to 40-50% of plot; **good seed production**; appearance of palatable species | ↑ Grass cover dominates majority of plot due to **seed bank; palatable grass species establish** | ↑ Further **grass seed bank build-up; grass dominance helps block invasives** to larger extent (total of 15-20 species) |
| Native shrubs / herbs / juvenile trees | ↓ Very **low species diversity and abundance** due to recruitment suppression | ↑ Emergence of **pioneer tree and shrub species** (normally 25-30 species); seed production increases | ↑ Emergence of successional tree and shrub species + herbaceous species (80-100 species) | ↑ Good diversity and abundance of shrub / juvenile tree species and herbaceous species (around 200 species) |
| Eupatorium/ Parthenium | ↓ Low presence due to **suppression by Lantana / Senna (except on road sides / fire lines)** | ↑ Strong **emergence in areas opened up** with Lantana /Senna removal, aided by absence of native plant species | ↓ **Gradual reduction** with domination by grasses / shrubs + removal activity | ↓ **Further reduction** with increase in native species; **risk of seed dispersal by roads /safari vehicles** |

**Note:** Management of secondary invasives requires increasing grass cover and seed bank of grasses and other pioneer species, as well as steps to avoid build-up of the seed bank of secondary invasives.

# ANNEXURE 4: BASELINE SURVEY-CUM-RESTORATION PLAN

## BASELINE PLOT SURVEY

| S No | Survey parameters | Metrics | Survey results |
|---|---|---|---|
| 1 | Plot terrain (dominant) | Hilly/flat/low lying | |
| 2 | Plot altitude | Metres | |
| 3 | Pre-existing vegetation | | |
| | Mature seed-bearing trees | Good/average/low | |
| | Juvenile trees | Good/average/low | |
| | Shrubs/herbs/other habits | Good/average/low | |
| | Grasses | Good/average/low | |
| 4 | Areas with denuded vegetation | High/moderate /low | |
| 5 | Presence of successional species | Good/average/low | |
| 6 | Soil condition | | |
| | Soil type (dominant) | (Typical soil types) | |
| | Soil compaction | Severe/moderate/ low | |
| | Soil organic content | Good/average/poor | |
| | Other soil indicators | | |
| 7 | Soil erosion | | |
| | Sheet erosion | Severe/moderate/ low | |
| | Gully erosion | Severe/moderate/ low | |
| | Moisture retention potential | Good/average/poor | |
| 8 | Streams / waterbodies | Yes / No | |

| 9 | Presence of invasive species | | |
|---|---|---|---|
| | Lantana camara | High/moderate /low | |
| | Senna spectabilis | High/moderate /low | |
| | Secondary invasive species | High/moderate /low | |
| 10 | Status of adjacent plots | Invaded / uninvaded | |
| 11 | Anthropogenic pressures | High/moderate /low | |
| 12 | Any other relevant aspects | | |

## RESTORATION PLAN

| S No | Activity | Restoration Plan |
|---|---|---|
| 1 | Lantana removal | |
| 2 | Removal of other invasive species | |
| 3 | Grass slip transplanting | |
| 4 | Grass seed dibbling | |
| 5 | Seed dibbling – other species | |
| 6 | Sapling planting | |
| 7 | Natural juvenile support | |
| 8 | Gully plugs / trenches | |
| 9 | Rock detention structures | |
| 10 | Other activities (list) | |

## ANNEXURE 5: CITATIONS

1-5. Workshop Manual: Eradication of Invasive Weeds and Habitat Restoration. Centre for Environmental Management of Degraded Ecosystems (CEMCE), University of Delhi, 2014

6. Johnson JH, Jensen JM. Hepatotoxicity and secondary photosensitization in a red kangaroo (Megaleia rufus) due to ingestion of Lantana camara. J Zoo Wildl Med. 1998 Jun;29(2):203-7. PMID: 9732038.

7. Sharma OP, Makkar HP, Dawra RK, Negi SS. A review of the toxicity of Lantana camara (Linn) in animals. Clin Toxicol. 1981 Sep;18(9):1077-94. doi: 10.3109/15563658108990337. PMID: 7032835.

8. LANTANA CAMARA: A TOXIC WEED IN LIVESTOCK DEVELOPMENT. (2023). *Indian Journal of Veterinary and Animal Sciences Research*, *51*(6), 1-10. https://epubs.icar.org.in/index.php/IJVASR/article/view/135319

9. Amit Love, Suresh Babu and C. R. Babu . Management of Lantana, an invasive alien weed, in forest ecosystems of India. Current Science, Vol. 97, no. 10, 25 November 2009

10. Ramesh Venkataraman, R. Sundararaju and Pranav Capila. Managing Invasives: Narratives Of Scale. *Sanctuary Asia*, Vol. 44 No. 2, February 2024

11. International principles and standards for the practice of ecological restoration. Society for Ecological Restoration. Second edition: September 2019

12. Maynard-Bean E, Kaye M. Invasive shrub removal benefits native plants in an eastern deciduous forest of North America. *Invasive Plant Science and Management*. 2019;12(1):3-10. doi:10.1017/inp.2018.35

13. Common Dryland Trees of Karnataka. Ashoka Trust for Research in Ecology and the Environment, 2012.

14. IUCN Guidelines for the Prevention of Biodiversity Loss Caused by Alien Invasive Species, February 2000.

15. Applied nucleation restoration guide for tropical forests. Conservation International, March 2021.

16. Standards of practice to guide ecosystem restoration: A contribution to the United Nations Decade on Ecosystem Restoration 2021–2030, Published by the Food and Agriculture Organization of the United Nations and the Society for Ecological Restoration and the International Union for Conservation of Nature Rome, Washington, DC and Gland, 2024

17. Schmitz, O.J., Sylvén, M., Atwood, T.B. *et al.* Trophic rewilding can expand natural climate solutions. *Nat. Clim. Chang.* 13, 324–333 (2023). https://doi.org/10.1038/s41558-023-01631-6

**Note on images, diagrams and photographs:**

Unless where specifically acknowledged, all images, videos, diagrams and photographs in this manual are from the archives of Junglescapes Charitable Trust.

The Junglescapes' team with the SER Full Circle Award 2017

*"The Society has selected Junglescapes for this award in recognition of the holistic and inclusive approach you have taken to facilitating the recovery of degraded forest ecosystems and vital habitat across a large area, and working closely and collaboratively with local communities in your efforts to do so"*

*- Society for Ecological Restoration*
*(Full Circe award citation 2017)*

# NOTES

# NOTES

# NOTES

# NOTES

# NOTES

# NOTES

# NOTES

www.ingramcontent.com/pod-product-compliance
Ingram Content Group UK Ltd.
Pitfield, Milton Keynes, MK11 3LW, UK
UKHW061027310726
14090UKWH00024B/443

* 9 7 9 8 8 9 5 4 4 7 5 0 5 *